My Secret List of Sites that Pay

Created by
J. Goldenberg
E. McNew
COPYRIGHT © 20.
FIRST PRINTING
February 1, 2014

ALL RIGHTS RESERVED. This book contains material protected under International and Federal Copyright Laws and Treaties. Any unauthorized reprint or use of this material is prohibited. No part of this book may be reproduced or transmitted in any form or by any means, electronic or mechanical, including photocopying, recording, or by any information storage and retrieval system without express written permission from the author / publisher.

CONTENTS

MY SECRET LIST OF SITES THAT PAY	1
DISCLAIMER	5
INTRODUCTION	7
WHAT DO YOU LOVE?	9
WHAT ARE YOU GOOD AT?	10
MY PASSION	13
ADVERTISING	15
BLOGGING	19
PUBLISHING YOUR OWN BOOKS	21
BECOME A LIVE EXPERT	25
GIVING ADVICE	29
OTHER ONLINE SITES	31
SUMMING IT UP	37

DISCLAIMER

This narrative is written to offer information and education to our readers. It is sold/uploaded with the understanding that the publisher and/or author is not engaged to render any type of psychological, legal, or any other kind of professional advice. This content is the sole expression and opinion of the author. Neither the publisher nor the individual author(s) shall be liable for any physical, psychological, emotional, financial, or commercial damages, including, but not limited to, special, incidental, consequential or other damages. Our views and rights are the same: You are responsible for your own choices, actions, and results.

Introduction

I clearly recall the frustration that I felt when I knew that there *had* to be a way to earn an income online, but I just didn't know *where* to go. I remember seeing a couple, as guests on a talk-show, who were livin' the life from their newfound cash flow. All from the web. They were so convincing, and excited! After watching an hour of their excitement, and getting pumped up myself, I was directed to "Sign up right away!" because it was a "Limited time offer!" Of course, I raced to my computer to log on. After spending ten minutes filling out my "application", I just about lost it when that big credit card logo was flashing in my face. *Only $99.* UGH. Sound familiar?

This guide was written and researched for this reason. Our time is valuable, and by reading this book, I can guarantee that you will save a tremendous amount of time. There are ways to begin your journey to financial freedom, but you better know where to go, like *really,* know where to go.

Not enough of us understand how truly easy it is to make extra money online. It's beyond frustrating making attempts to find reliable online companies who will pay you without asking for X amount of money for "memberships" and the like. If this ever happens, RED FLAG.

What I love about working online is the fact that it just takes a few clicks in your spare time to get started, and once you become established, which doesn't take long, you will have the freedom to choose your own schedule. You are looking at the PERFECT book to gather information to make money off of this never-ending, always growing place we call the internet.

You first have to figure out what you love doing best while online. Nothing in life is free, and in order to see profit, it does take some work. Before reading on to the resources I am about to offer, think about discovering what you are passionate about. It will make all the world of difference when you decide on which outlet(s) to take on the web. Most of the time, the simplest, easiest answers are right in front of us. We just need to stop looking in the wrong places to notice them.

What do you love?

Nothing is ever free, and nothing good will ever be easy. This reminds me of a saying; it's easier to take the "easy way out". Well, for one thing that doesn't even make sense. That is like saying "It's fun because it's fun". Well of course. But really, what is easy? In terms of giving up, is easy browsing around and typing in your email address hoping you'll get rich? Is easy signing up with a "free" site only to find out you have to pay $100? Is easy just running away from your "problems" because you are stressed out and can't quite figure out how to handle them?

Honestly, in my opinion none of that sounds very easy. And from my personal experience, it isn't. We look around at those who have it all, the car, the house, the family, the money, and we think to ourselves, "Well don't they have it easy." When in reality, the majority of these people have worked pretty darn hard to arrive at their "easy" place in life.

So really, we are totally confused and making contradictory statements regarding the word easy. Easy should be redefined. Easy should be viewed as what we love, what comes natural to us, what others praise us for, and what we excel at.

What are you good at?

For me, easy is my PASSION. I went my entire life knowing what I was good at, and knowing what came natural to me. When life happened, my self-doubt took over and told me that it could never become a reality. I would think, "Writers are boring. Yeah I'm alright at it, but who really makes a living off of that?" I convinced myself that the only thing that I was good at didn't really matter, and that no one would care about what I had to say anyway. Turns out, if you can successfully write a paper on, say…laundry detergent, or your favorite ice cream shop…you can apply this to the web in more ways than you think, and actually make cash from it!

The universe works in amazing (and sometimes tragic) ways. If we aren't living our lives doing what we are meant to be doing, and what we were essentially created to bring to the planet, the universe is going to let us know. Nothing will be working in our favor, nothing will ever seem to go right, and we will exist in a miserable robotic lifestyle. Let's compare this to a romantic relationship. We go out on our first date, the total unknown. Of course, it is easy to fantasize and hope for the best, "maybe I'll meet my future husband/wife" we think. It turns out that this date is a total bomber, boring, and completely incompatible with who we are. What is going to happen if we continue to entertain this relationship based on hopes? We'll be miserable, stuck in the same place we were last year, and continue to "hope" that it will work out.

Turn the tables, we actually do meet the love of our life! The only result would be inner peace, happiness, and content knowing that we are with who we are supposed to be with!

The same goes for our passion, or our "easy". To stay around at that job "hoping" to get a life-changing raise, or to spend the rest of your life living in that smog-filled city because there is more opportunity for a "maybe", just does not make sense!

Your passion is that humble, silent voice inside of your subconscious. Your passion is that one thing that your heart is always nagging you about. Your passion emerges when you put yourself into action and face change with real, honest faith; not "hope".

From the age of twelve, I was always searching for what I really wanted to do in life. I took into consideration the money first, and what I loved second.

My passion was with me all along. I wrote my first poem when I was only ten. I made awesome grades in English classes. Everyone around me was constantly asking me why I wasn't writing more.

I didn't think it was the cool thing to do. I went to college for nursing school, got involved with the wrong person, and the universe pretty much forced me to live out an insane story to one day write about. Nothing went my way, and for a now twenty-six year old, I have so many things to write about that I could not even possibly fit it all into one novel. (You can find part one at the end of this guide.)

Trusting in the universe, and trusting that the universe will lead you to find your self-fulfilling purpose in life is the first step on that ladder of true life. True living. True happiness. True content.

We cannot ever discover our passion by consciously searching for it. It comes with action. Trial and error, and getting the courage to step outside of our comfort zone. The most talented people have one thing in common; they do not believe that they are even good at what they do! How can we possibly ever even know, if we don't try? Every living creature has a purpose, and every living creature has a passion. It is a matter of letting go, not letting yourself worry if you're good enough, and freeing yourself to be WHO YOU ARE.

Every trial in life has a purpose. These trials are an attempt to point you in the right direction.

The possibilities are endless. For this reason, I hope that you finish this message with a new sense of who you are, and who you are meant to be. Just let go, keep your mind open, and know that the universe has your back. Now quit whining and take action.

Let's move on and get you signed up with some reliable and awesome websites.

Advertising

Advertising isn't always what it sounds like. When I first began my journey into making a living online, I had no knowledge of advertising, period. Don't let yourself think negative thoughts or doubt yourself, because the following websites make their opportunities extremely simple and easy to follow. It's a matter of practice and repetition. If everything looks totally foreign at first, don't let it scare you off. You will pick up on it quicker than you think. This is a learning process. If you really want to work for yourself, stick it out and you won't regret it.

First, register with an Affiliate network. What happens with this, is you choose a legit business to advertise for, and promote their products using external links and banners that they provide. You can post these links anywhere that you please, as long as the third party site isn't opposed, of course. If you have your own website or blog, it's a great place to start. Each person that clicks on your link and signs on with the company, or buys a product, will make you money. Below is a list of reputable websites who genuinely pay well and make your effort worth-while.

1) Amazon Associates

I personally work for Amazon Associates, and I love the freedom they offer by giving you so many different choices on how you can advertise. You can choose virtually any product on Amazon to advertise, and you can also open your own web store, selling their products for commission. You can find all of the details by going to this address.

https://affiliate-program.amazon.com

This is what they have to say:

"Use our Site Stripe toolbar to easily add links and for a quick view of your earnings:

Link to any Page

Navigate to any Amazon product details page and capture the links directly from page you are viewing.

Build Slideshows on the Fly

Add a product to an Amazon widget directly from a product detail page. Create a new widget or update an existing one. Supports Carousel, My Favorites, Slideshow and MP3 Clips widgets.

Share on Twitter and Facebook

Post a quick update to Facebook or Twitter with a link to the Amazon page you are viewing

View Earnings Summary

See your earnings report from your Site Stripe Toolbar."

They literally give you step-by-step instructions. Amazon is one of the most customer and affiliate-friendly company that you will come across. To find out more on what they offer, just scroll all the way down to the bottom of the page, and check out those tiny links.

2) Just Answer

This is another website that is great, and can work for you in three ways;

Advertising

Referrals

Giving professional advice

http://www.justanswer.com/professional

This is what they have to say:

"We invite you to join a community of professionals who answer questions on JustAnswer and Pearl.com. You will answer questions on your own time, and get paid by our rapidly growing customer base of more than 20 million people and counting.

To join the community of professionals, you will need to:

Complete an online application and online profile

Take a short subject matter test

Verify your credentials

Any license or certification,

- 2+ years of research-related employment (e.g. librarian, analyst),
- Or a Bachelor's degree or higher.

Don't see a category for your expertise?

Start a new category for your area of knowledge. As a founding professional for a new category, you will not need to report your credentials just yet."

3) Commission Junction

This site also has several options from affiliate advertising to pay-per-call advertising. Lots of different outlets. You can also earn referral fees for sending your friends, or anyone else (possibly your blog-readers!) to sign up. It's so simple; blog about all of the different opportunities you have discovered online, paste your tracking link (provided by the website) to direct your readers to your sources, and presto!

http://www.cj.com/what-is-affiliate-marketing

4) Max Bounty

Another site based on advertising, but they also include high bonuses and referral offers as well. I encourage you to check out each and every one of these links. Every person has something unique to offer, and you don't want to miss out on what could be a great opportunity.

http://www.maxbounty.com/

5) Info Links

Info links has all of the above, as well as an advanced system in place to tell you what is working successfully and what is not. This is one of the many different outlets offered to help you track your progress, impressions, clicks, and conversions.

http://infolinks.com

Blogging

If you love to write, and want to make money doing it, this is for you. Basically, you get paid to write for the areas of service/expertise for thriving websites, submit product reviews, or pretty much whatever floats you're boat. There are tons of third party sites that will pay you to advertise their product on your blog. You can first set up your blog with the following;

6) YouTube
 Of course, this is mostly video blogging. You can create your video, add your tags, and "monetize" your video. YouTube does its magic and finds a suitable advertising biz to place ads before your video starts. If you have enough traffic and videos, this can definitely add up!
www.youtube.com
Check out my silly YouTube channel here
http://bit.ly/1fslFaY

7) Google blogger
Personally, I have seen the best results from google blogger. I get at least forty percent more clicks than I would from other media outlets. Google+ is a great place to start your blog, and it is extremely easy to get it noticed. When your finished blogging, simply tag people in your circles who you think may be interested in reading about what you have to say. This gives your work *tons* of exposure.
www.blogger.com

*The random thoughts of your crazy author (me) **http://bit.ly/1dVeR6m**

Publishing your own books, guides, or blogs

8) KDP Select

My favorite for obvious reasons, if you have any quality piece of content via articles or full novels, you can publish them to KDP for free and start earning royalties up to 70%. I honestly wish I had known about KDP much earlier. KDP will give you free promotion days, and they have a new countdown deal in place as well. For authors, in my opinion, KDP is even better than traditional publishing. You can go straight to this link or check it out next time you're browsing Amazon.

https://kdp.amazon.com/self-publishing/KDPSelect

From Amazon.com, scroll all the way down to where it says "self-publish with us" and click. You will be directed to set up your account which is just your basic information and payment info for royalties. When you are ready to release a book, or even if you are still in progress, click the "create title" icon and it will prompt you to add the information, title, and cover. If you do not have a pre-made cover, KDP gives you a selection to choose from and allows you to choose specific formatting. They look very professional and the best part is that they're totally free, including the high-quality stock images.

This can get extremely addicting so I caution you. Also, this is one of those things where you aren't going to become a millionaire overnight. You have to study the website, learn the program, and spend months and months of trial and error until you have it right. Some of my favorite books for learning how to publish with KDP are **The kindle Publishing Bible** by Tom Corson-Knowles, and **Make a Killing on Kindle** by Michael Alvear. I have read all of what is out there under this topic, and these two books offered me the best information.

*My best-selling memoir (sometimes, that is) *Testing the Waters* can be found by clicking here:
http://amzn.to/18fhs5m

9) WiseBread
One of the best places to blog about *anything finance*. If you have an interest for stocks, what's new with the economy, or you just love money, and everything there is to learn and share, check it out.
http://WiseBread.com
Also, once your blog is up and running, you are going to want to register with **Google AdSense**, which is kind of like a digital advertising swap meet of some sort. You'll paste an HTML code that they will provide to you, on your blog, or any other content, and it pretty much gives them permission to post ads up on your site. When someone clicks and participates/purchases the service, you get paid. You can do this by going to the URL below.
www.google.com/adsense
Google Analytics is also a great resource. It is easy to sign up (just use your Gmail account), and they allow you to thoroughly track your ads, how many clicks they receive, and where the clicks are coming from. This information allows you to get an idea of what is worth your time and what is not making a profit. You will find this website by going to the address below.
http://www.google.com/analytics

Become a live expert

If you feel that you have what it takes to become a live expert in virtually any area of your knowledge, fill out an application at one (or all) of the locations below. If you would love to make extra cash advising customers with your skill, talent, or knowledge via live chat, video chat, or even just through email, this is probably an awesome opportunity for you. The sites below are sites that I have enrolled in, and tested. Obviously, you will need to stay consistent if you want to make any real money, but the good news is that most of the live chat opportunities allow you to choose **your own price per minute**. You can do this however is best suited for you. If you love talking in person with strangers about their life dilemmas, then do live webcam counseling sessions. If you really don't want to see or hear the person on the other end, offer services via email.

Now, as far as giving advice via live chat or video chat, this is really only a good fit for a person who is confident with their skills and not afraid to stand their ground if necessary. You will be speaking with random people across the globe on a daily basis, (of course getting paid), Just make sure that you know what you are getting into before diving right in. For all the ladies out there, who see those ads for "webcam models", or "make money flirting" I hope you know what this *really* is. It's an invitation to strip down for some of the most disturbing people that the planet can offer. Beware. But of course, to each their own.

10) Be a Guide

Here you can charge what you want, and *per* question asked. Trust me when I say, there is just about a category for any person to be an *expert* in. If you can't find your specific category, they will give you the option to submit a request to implement your specific category.

http://BeAguide.about.com

11) Yahoo Contributor Network

If you love writing articles and essays, sign up here and test your luck! I have published several articles here, and most all of them offer performance pay, meaning that you get paid per visitor. It is not very much money unless you can generate a lot of traffic and write a lot of articles; but it is fun and great practice. The articles that I usually go for are the ones up for grabs that offer the up-front pay which usually ranges from $10-$50. The most common is $10, though. If you are an expert in an area that they are needing submissions for, it should only take a few minutes to write a quick essay and make the quick cash. I recently wrote an article that they actually asked me to do on the crazy weather we've been having this year. You can read it here if you want to see what your article will look like. Just scroll down my Yahoo contributor profile until you find it:

http://yhoo.it/LH76X8

Click below to get started!
http://contributor.yahoo.com/join//?refer=1773715

Giving Advice

Believe it or not, you can actually make money giving advice online. This can range from topics such as cooking, mental health, family relationships, pretty much anything you can think of. And what's really cool is that on most sites you don't have to have any special set of credentials or education. Below is a list of awesome sites that I have personally checked out.

12) www.SmallBizAdvice.com (Small business advice)

13) www.Keen.com (Are you psychic??)

14) www.WeRLive.com (A personal favorite, advice you can give on pretty much anything)

15) www.Ammas.com (another one with endless possibilities)

16) www.ChaCha.com (Advice via mobile!)

17) www.JustAsk.com (pretty much explains itself)

Other online sites I recommend checking out:

18) Cash Back Research
They emphasize that you won't get rich, but they really do pay you for taking their surveys! (Hey, at least they're honest!)
http://www.cashbackresearch.com/doi/index.asp?utm_campaign=HomeSurveys

19) Live Ops
These guys have over 20,000 agents working for them, from home. As an employee, you'll take incoming calls for their affiliate corporations. The company provides training, and as many (or little) hours as you want. For this you will need to have the proper set-up at home. A high-speed computer and internet, reserved time where there will be no background noise or distraction, a designated office space dedicated to only working, etcetera.
http://LiveOps.com

Definitely don't get too excited with the idea that working for an online biz won't be work, because it will. And don't come to the assumption that you can do this kind of work while taking care of your small kids who scream bloody murder when they bonk their fuzzy little heads on the coffee table. It needs to be the professional and courteous environment in which you would get by calling any major company as a paying customer (wireless, banking, cable television). When you pick up the phone; to rip your wireless carrier a new one for those random and unexpected fees, there is a good chance that you are speaking to a representative who is working from their own home (believe it or not). Now, imagine if you suddenly heard a screaming child in the background, as you were trying to pay your bill or solve a conflict.

I can just picture the hilarious and awkward outcome…

"Ma'am, can you please hold for a moment?" She politely asks in her sweet telemarketing and well-trained tone. "JOHNNY!!! WHAT DID I TELL YOU ABOUT POURING DISH SOAP ON THE KITCHEN FLOOR! Oh no! Your nose is bleeding! JOHNNY…!"

I couldn't help myself. On to the last five.

20) Government telework

This is the governments' attempt to provide job security, and apparently its working!

http://TeleWork.gov

21) Sales Roads

Work from home, set appointments, and generate leads. They offer great commission. I am guessing that some experience would be desired, but I am not positive.

http://Salesroads.com

22) Why, **eBay** of course!

Why do people think that it's some sort of big deal to set up a seller account with eBay!? You don't even have to sell anything, you just need the product. EBay will do the rest for you, and if you price your stuff right, or at least fair, you'll be surprised at how fast someone will click that *BUY NOW* button. The only things that you'll need is a PayPal account and an email address. And obviously, something to sell. Take into consideration the fact that people are selling pictures of their feet, or even an inappropriately shaped Cheetos. Just sayin', you can pretty much sell anything. EBay has a special category of "other" items, with sub-categories of "Weird", "Really weird" and "Completely bizarre". EBay isn't just for finding Prada bags and pretty jewelry. You will find everything from shrunken heads, to "bird poop remover for your car" to a bag of Chex mix for $29. Seriously.

www.ebay.com

You can easily go through your closet and find at least five things that someone will want to buy. Those shoes that you never wear, the hideous floral muumuu that your great-grandma gifted to you last Christmas, or the childhood BB-gun that gets you screamed at every time you pretend-shoot your wife. If you don't believe me, go ahead and see for yourself.

23) AR Recovery

For those who are familiar in the medical field, you can work at home by taking calls, answering questions, and assisting with payment plans.

<u>This is what they have to say</u>:

"If you're an expert in healthcare receivables, self-directed and motivated, highly ethical, professional, and ready to be rewarded for your hard work, then A/R Recovery might be what you're looking for. At A/R Recovery, you'll be working with people who are experts at what they do and who love their work. You'll be paid well and receive a bonus for producing the desired results. You may have the option to work from your own home.

Our work environment is casual and flexible, allowing people to balance their dedication to their work with the other commitments in their lives. In recognition of the expertise and motivation that characterize A/R Recovery employees, the compensation at A/R Recovery is above average and includes benefits such as paid vacation and a 401(k) plan."

24) Fiverr

This website is one of my current favorites. It's amazing what people will do for $5. But also, it's amazing what you, as a seller, can SELL for $5! You have to check it out to understand what I'm talking about. You can literally get paid for anything. From writing a business name on your forehead to editing another author's work, the possibilities are endless. People get paid to write a message on a piece of toast with mustard, to say "Happy Birthday" for a customers' brother, or advertise a logo for a biz…Yeah…

*Find me, and gigs here, from reviews to video advertising to book covers. It really makes $!
http://bit.ly/1kYOKkz

Or, Just go here and sign yourself up:
http://www.fiverr.com

25) ACX

This is an audio book exchange site. You can log in and browse around for current authors, who are posting auditions for a good voice to narrate and record their content. If you're comfortable with speaking into a recording device, go for it! You will send the author a fifteen minute audition, and if they like what they hear than they will accept your offer to do the entire novel. You will get paid through charging per hour of recording, or splitting the sales in royalties of 50/50. This second option would be a great idea for long-term income. If you did this for multiple books, you would be getting paychecks over time indefinitely, for a possibly nice amount! $$$

http://acx.com

Summing it up

There are PLENTY of ways to make money online. And it's so simple. It's about finding a reputable, legitimate company to work with. Of course you will have to put in some effort, but if you're lazy like me, and want to work on your own schedule, I suggest checking out all of these links above. Keep in mind that your online income is not going to find you. You are the one responsible for finding your online income! With plenty of patience, time and research, I am 100% sure that you can do this well. Just remember to stay consistent and do your homework. I hope this helps you find your share of financial freedom. Good luck!

J. GOLDENBERG

E. McNew

For updates on future publications, send "UPDATES" in the subject line to **mcnewpublishing@gmail.com**

www.ingramcontent.com/pod-product-compliance
Lightning Source LLC
Chambersburg PA
CBHW051826170526
45167CB00005B/2174